Test Booklet 2

Third Edition

# Person to Person

## Communicative Speaking and Listening Skills

Jack C. Richards David Bycina Ingrid Wisniewska
Andy London

OXFORD
UNIVERSITY PRESS

198 Madison Avenue
New York, NY 10016 USA

Great Clarendon Street, Oxford OX2 6DP UK

Oxford University Press is a department of the University of Oxford.
It furthers the University's objective of excellence in research, scholarship,
and education by publishing worldwide in

Oxford New York

Auckland Cape Town Dar es Salaam Hong Kong Karachi
Kuala Lumpur Madrid Melbourne Mexico City Nairobi
New Delhi Shanghai Taipei Toronto

With offices in

Argentina Austria Brazil Chile Czech Republic France Greece
Guatemala Hungary Italy Japan Poland Portugal Singapore
South Korea Switzerland Thailand Turkey Ukraine Vietnam



Executive Publisher: Nancy Leonhardt
Senior Acquisitions Editor: Chris Balderston
Senior Editor: Patricia O'Neill
Associate Editor: Amy E. Hawley
Assistant Editor: Kate Schubert
Art Director: Maj-Britt Hagsted
Layout Artist: Elizabeth Onorato
Production Manager: Shanta Persaud
Production Controller: Eve Wong

ISBN-13: 978 0 19 430231 9 (Test Booklet 2)
ISBN-10: 0 19 430231 8 (Test Booklet 2)

ISBN-13: 978 0 19 430230 2 (Test Booklet 2 with CD)
ISBN-10: 0 19 430230 X (Test Booklet 2 with CD)

Printed in Hong Kong.

10 9 8 7 6 5 4 3 2 1

# CONTENTS

# INTRODUCTION

*Person to Person, 3rd edition, Test Booklet 2* is designed for unit-by-unit evaluation of students' mastery of the Student Book. The tests may be given in a language laboratory or in a regular classroom with a CD player, and they are easily administered to large or small groups of students. Teachers may use the tests to assign grades or to identify areas in which students need additional assistance.

This test package includes photocopiable student test sheets, an answer key, and an audio script of the recorded portions of the tests. A CD on the inside back cover of the Test Booklet contains the recordings needed to administer the tests.

The test items are based on the listening and speaking activities presented in the Student Book. Listen to This assesses listening ability, while Give It A Try assesses speaking ability. Both sections are presented in multiple-choice, true-false, or matching formats.

## The Tests

Each unit test is divided into two sections and is worth a total of 20 points. This format was chosen to make it easier for teachers of large classes to administer and score their students' tests.

The tests can be adapted according to the needs of the teacher and students. Teachers may wish to use only certain sections of a test because of time constraints. It may also be appropriate in some cases to play one part of a test twice, depending on the students' level and the intended use of the test results.

## Timing

Each unit test is about 10-15 minutes long. Actual administration time, including set-up and collection of materials at the end of the test, may run ten minutes longer.

## Giving the Test

Before the students arrive, teachers should photocopy test sheets for themselves and all of their students. When the class has started, teachers distribute the test sheets and have the students write their names and the date on them. Teachers then read aloud the instructions for the first section and play the CD. (They may wish to play each recording twice.) Before playing the second section, teachers should go over the instructions and make sure students understand them. Once the listening section is completed, teachers can then have students complete the speaking section. This section presents the language and functions practiced in the Student Book, and students select the answer that best completes the sample conversation. When the test is finished, teachers collect the test sheets from the class. They should check to make sure they receive one test sheet from each student and that each test sheet has the correct name written on it.

## Scoring

Space is provided at the end of each section to write the students' scores for that section. In addition, space is provided at the top of the test sheet to write the students' total score. A scale of 20 points is used to make it easy to convert the scores to grades.

Teachers may wish to go over the test in class so that students can see their errors and review any difficult areas. The test results can help teachers determine where additional practice is needed. When assigning grades, it is most beneficial to use the test results in conjunction with other types of assessment, such as the speaking activities in the Let's Talk sections of the Student Book. A wide variety of assessments will give teachers a fuller picture of their students' skills and strengths.

# Unit 1 Test

TOTAL SCORE ___ 20

Name: ______________________ Date: ____________

## LISTEN TO THIS

Track 2

**1. People are talking. Listen and circle the letter of the correct answer.**

1. a. They are talking at a diner.
   b. They are talking at a picnic.
   c. They are talking at City College.

2. a. Christine said the hot dogs taste delicious.
   b. Christine said the Greek salad tastes delicious.
   c. Christine said the water tastes delicious.

3. a. Doug works as a server.
   b. Christine works as a server.
   c. They both work as servers.

4. a. They know each other from college.
   b. They know each other from the picnic.
   c. They know each other from a diner.

5. a. Doug usually wears a suit.
   b. Doug orders an iced tea every Wednesday.
   c. Doug works across the street from City College.

___ 5

Track 3

**2. People are talking. Are these statements true or false? Listen and check (✓) the correct answer.**

| | True | False |
|---|---|---|
| 1. Mariko heard so much about Alex. | ☐ | ☐ |
| 2. Sally introduced Mariko and Alex. | ☐ | ☐ |
| 3. Mariko just came back from Brazil. | ☐ | ☐ |
| 4. Alex dances whenever he can. | ☐ | ☐ |
| 5. Alex invited Mariko to go dancing. | ☐ | ☐ |

___ 5

## GIVE IT A TRY

**1. Find the definition for each expression and circle the letter of the correct answer.**

1. *This is a great place, isn't it* means
   a. I'm not sure if this is a great place.
   b. I think this is a great place.
   c. I think this isn't a great place.

2. *Haven't we met before* means
   a. I think we've met before.
   b. I don't think we've met before.
   c. I think we've never met before.

3. *This is my first time* means
   a. I've done this before.
   b. I want to do this.
   c. I haven't done this before.

4. *I'm not bad* means
   a. I have some talent.
   b. I'm not talented.
   c. I'm really talented.

5. *Sounds cool* means
   a. it doesn't interest me.
   b. it's going to be chilly.
   c. it interests me a lot.

5

**2. Complete each sentence with the letter of the correct answer.**

1. I ________________ you are a good student.
   a. hearing
   b. hear
   c. listen

2. Hello, Jung-mo. I'm ________________ to meet you.
   a. good
   b. nice
   c. glad

3. I just came ________________ Spain.
   a. at
   b. back
   c. back from

4. I love music, especially ________________.
   a. rock
   b. yoga
   c. judo

5. I don't know you. I think you have ________________ person.
   a. the right
   b. the wrong
   c. another

5

# Unit 2 Test

TOTAL SCORE ___ 20

Name: ______________________ Date: __________

## LISTEN TO THIS

Track 4

**1. People are asking where they can run errands. Listen and write the letter of the correct answer.**

1. buy some fresh vegetables ___
2. check e-mail ___
3. go to a dry cleaner's ___
4. buy some aspirin ___
5. mail a package ___

a. behind the pharmacy
b. in the shopping mall
c. next to that tall building
d. about three blocks from here
e. on the corner

___ 5

Track 5

**2. People are asking where they can find things in an art museum. Listen and write the letter of the correct answer.**

1. The gift shop is ___
2. The bathroom is ___
3. European paintings are ___
4. The exit is ___
5. The Egyptian art is ___

a. on the third floor.
b. on the lower level. Take the elevator down one flight.
c. straight ahead, about three rooms down.
d. on the second floor.
e. on the ground floor.

___ 5

## GIVE IT A TRY

**1. Complete each sentence with the letter of the correct answer.**

1. A: ______________! Oh no, you got mustard on your shirt.
   B: Do you know where I can get it cleaned?

   a. Watch up
   b. Be caring
   c. Watch out

2. A: ________________! I broke my watch! What am I going to do now?
   B: You can buy a new one at the mall.

   a. I'm just lucky
   b. Just my luck
   c. Just in the luck

3. A: Hi. Can ________________?
   B: Yes. Is there a music shop around here?

   a. I help you
   b. you help me
   c. you help us

4. A: Excuse me. Where can I find a bank?
   B: There's one two stores ________________.

   a. near
   b. around
   c. down

5. A: Can you tell me where the exit is, please?
   B: ________________ the escalator up two flights.

   a. Make
   b. Take
   c. Get

5

**2. Complete each sentence with the letter of the correct answer.**

| | |
|---|---|
| 1. People put ___ on their feet. | a. wallet |
| 2. Last winter Li Ming wore ___ around her neck everyday. | b. a tie |
| 3. Billy keeps his money in his ___. | c. gloves |
| 4. I put on ___ when I wear my business suit. | d. a scarf |
| 5. When it's cold out, it's good to put ___ on your hands. | e. socks |

5

# Unit 3 Test

TOTAL SCORE ___ 20

Name: ______________________ Date: ___________

## LISTEN TO THIS

Track 6

**1. People are leaving messages. Listen and write the letter of the correct answer.**

1. Adam ___
2. Jimmy ___
3. Laura ___
4. Ellen ___
5. Mrs. Simpson ___

a. Could you tell him I'm angry at him for not calling me back?
b. Can you tell Fran I can't pick her up tomorrow?
c. I'm calling to tell him there's no school tomorrow.
d. Just tell her to call me back when she gets a chance.
e. Could you tell Andy I'm having a birthday party next Friday at my place at 8:00?

___ 5

Track 7

**2. A man is applying for a job. What does the receptionist tell him he must do? Listen and check (✓) the correct answer.**

| | Must | Doesn't have to |
|---|---|---|
| 1. fill out and send an application form | | |
| 2. tell the receptionist his zip code | | |
| 3. send a recommendation letter | | |
| 4. come to the store to get an application form | | |
| 5. call Charles back later | | |

___ 5

## GIVE IT A TRY

**1. Complete each conversation and circle the letter of the correct answer.**

1. A: Good morning. Admissions office. Can I help you?
   B: _______________?

   a. Can I take a message
   b. Can you tell me how to apply for a class
   c. Can I have your number

2. A: ________________?
   B: It's R-i-c-h-a-r-d B-o-x.

   a. Could I have your address
   b. Could you spell that, please
   c. Is Richard there, please

3. A: You just need to fill out an application form and send it to us.
   B: ________________?

   a. Can you tell me how to apply for a class
   b. Can I take a class
   c. Can you send me a form, please

4. A: Great. Could you send me a form, please?
   B: OK. ________________.

   a. I'll need your address
   b. I'll put you through
   c. You just need to fill out an application form

5. A: Hold on, please. I'll see if she's available...________________.
   B: OK. I'll call back later.

   a. I'm sorry, she is available right now
   b. I'm sorry, her line is busy right now
   c. I'll see she gets back to you very soon

( ) 5

**2. Read each sentence and choose the correct response. Write the letter of the correct answer.**

1. I need that package by tomorrow. ____
2. Can I take a message? ____
3. Thank you for all your help. ____
4. Can I apply to your school? ____
5. Is Jack there? ____

a. Don't mention it.
b. Yes, you just need to fill out an application form.
c. We'll send that out right away.
d. I'm sorry, he's busy.
e. Yes, could you ask him to call Dan?

( ) 5

# Unit 4 Test

TOTAL SCORE ____ 20

Name: ______________________ Date: ____________

## LISTEN TO THIS

Track 8

**1. People are complaining and offering suggestions. Listen and write the letter of the correct answer.**

1. The school bookstore can have a book sale. ____
2. Let's call the police and complain that there's too much noise. ____
3. If your cell phone rings, you fail the class. ____
4. You can set a time limit. ____
5. Let's start bringing our own lunch. ____

a. That's too risky.
b. Good idea.
c. That sounds great!
d. Leave it to you to think of that.
e. That wouldn't work. It's not fair.

5

Track 9

**2. People are complaining about their brothers. Listen and write the letter of the correct answer.**

1. George ____
2. Stan ____
3. Wilbur ____
4. Fred ____
5. Danny ____

a. I suppose you should tell him he's cheap.
b. If I were you, I'd tell him it's dangerous.
c. Why don't you ask him to play outside?
d. In that case, I think you should tell him to take singing lessons.
e. Why don't you tell him he's not funny and ask him to stop embarrassing you in front of your friends?

5

## GIVE IT A TRY

**1. Match the complaints with the suggestions. Write the letter of the correct answer.**

1. My roommate's stereo is always so loud. ____
2. I can't do anything. My father is too strict. ____
3. I'm gaining so much weight, my clothes don't fit. ____
4. I might fail my math class. ____
5. My boyfriend is so cheap. ____

a. study more
b. buy earplugs
c. break up with him
d. go on a diet
e. tell him to change his rules

5

## 2. Complete each conversation and circle the letter of the correct answer.

1. A: What's the matter?
   B: My boyfriend is so cheap! _______________?

   a. What's the problem
   b. What did he do
   c. What should I do

2. A: My mother is so strict. _______________.
   B: You should really talk to her about it.

   a. I don't know how to do it
   b. I don't know what to do
   c. I don't know anything

3. A: My sister snores. It's really annoying.
   B: _______________, I think you should wake her up.

   a. In that case
   b. By that case
   c. On that case

4. A: I saw my boyfriend holding someone else's hand. Now I'm so upset.
   B: _______________, I'd break up with him right away.

   a. If I knew you
   b. If you were me
   c. If I were you

5. A: You should tell him to exercise.
   B: _______________. If I criticize him, he gets angry at me.

   a. That's good
   b. That wouldn't work
   c. I suppose I should

5

# Unit 5 Test

TOTAL SCORE ___ 20

Name: ______________________ Date: __________

## LISTEN TO THIS

Track 10

**1. People are talking about what happened to their friends. Are these statements true or false? Listen and check (✓) the correct answer.**

| | True | False |
|---|---|---|
| 1. Soo-jung has her own TV show. | ☐ | ☐ |
| 2. Valerie is going back to college. | ☐ | ☐ |
| 3. Hyun-jin was in a car accident. | ☐ | ☐ |
| 4. Anna broke her ankle. | ☐ | ☐ |
| 5. Paul is going to study law. | ☐ | ☐ |

___ 5

Track 11

**2. People are talking about things that happened to their friends. Listen and write the letter of the correct answer.**

1. Becky ___ a. He should have been more careful.
2. Sean ___ b. He should have checked first.
3. Takeshi ___ c. He should have managed his time better.
4. Nancy ___ d. She should have driven slower.
5. Phil ___ e. She should have set her alarm clock.

___ 5

## GIVE IT A TRY

**1. Two people are talking about their friend Joey. Number the sentences in the correct order.**

1. ___ A: He broke his arm, but he'll be fine.
2. ___ A: He fell asleep while driving and crashed into a tree.
3. ___ B: No, what happened?
4. ___ A: Did you hear about Joey?
5. ___ B: Poor Joey! Was he hurt?

___ 5

**2.** **Find the definition for each expression and circle the letter of the correct answer.**

1. *Let me get this straight* means
   a. let me fix it.
   b. let me find something straight.
   c. let me understand what you just said.

2. *How are things with her* means
   a. how are her things.
   b. how is she doing.
   c. how is she doing things.

3. *Well, so-so* means
   a. really good.
   b. bad.
   c. OK.

4. *She ended up in the hospital* means
   a. however, she went to the hospital.
   b. as a result, she went to the hospital.
   c. in addition, she went to the hospital.

5. *I hope it works out well for you* means
   a. I hope you work hard at it.
   b. I hope you exercise well.
   c. I hope you succeed at it.

___ 5

# Unit 6 Test

TOTAL SCORE ___ 20

Name: ______________________ Date: ____________

## LISTEN TO THIS

Track 12

**1. A man is talking to his coworker. Listen and write the letter of the correct answer.**

1. Are you OK? ___
2. What's the matter? ___
3. Did you take anything for it? ___
4. Why didn't you call a doctor? ___
5. Why don't you go home? ___

a. But I have an important meeting in a few minutes!
b. I thought I might feel better in a few hours.
c. I have an awful backache.
d. I took some aspirin but it didn't help at all.
e. To tell you the truth, I don't feel very well.

___ 5

Track 13

**2. A person is talking to a pharmacist. Listen and write the letter of the correct answer.**

1. She ___ take one tablet every four to six hours.
2. She ___ take it with food.
3. She ___ take any aspirin.
4. She ___ have tea.
5. She ___ see a doctor.

a. shouldn't
b. had better
c. must
d. should
e. can

___ 5

## GIVE IT A TRY

**1. Read each question and choose the correct response. Circle the letter of the correct answer.**

1. You look feverish. Are you OK?
   a. Yes, I have a cold.
   b. To tell you the truth, I feel terrible.
   c. Yes, that's a good idea.

2. Are there any special instructions?
   a. Yes, I have a headache.
   b. Yes, you must take these with food.
   c. Yes, I think I have a cold.

3. What are your symptoms?
   a. I have a fever and a bad cough.
   b. I am allergic to aspirin.
   c. I took some medicine, but it didn't do any good.

4. Are you allergic to anything?
   a. Yes, I have a terrible toothache.
   b. Yes, aspirin.
   c. Yes, a backache.

5. What do you recommend for a sore throat?
   a. I recommend these eye drops.
   b. You could have bad allergies.
   c. You could try this medicine.

5

**2. Are the definitions of these expressions true or false? Check (✓) the correct answer.**

| | True | False |
|---|---|---|
| 1. *If your fever doesn't come down* means if you continue to have a fever. | ☐ | ☐ |
| 2. *There's a pretty bad flu going around* means many people have not gotten the flu. | ☐ | ☐ |
| 3. *I might feel better after a good night's sleep* means I might feel better in the morning. | ☐ | ☐ |
| 4. *The aspirin didn't do any good* means the aspirin didn't help. | ☐ | ☐ |
| 5. *I twisted my ankle* means the bone in my ankle is broken. | ☐ | ☐ |

5

# Unit 7 Test

TOTAL SCORE ___ 20

Name: ______________________ Date: ________

## LISTEN TO THIS

Track 14

**1. A person is explaining a cheesecake recipe. Listen to the instructions and then number the sentences in the correct order.**

1. ___ Pour the other ingredients over it.
2. ___ Put the graham crackers in the pan and break them into very small pieces.
3. ___ Put it into the oven and bake it for 40 minutes at 230 degrees.
4. ___ Put the cream cheese, eggs, sugar, vanilla extract, and heavy cream into a bowl.
5. ___ Mix it all together until it's smooth and creamy.

___ 5

Track 15

**2. People are talking about going on a trip. What does Yoshi need to bring and why? Listen and write the letter of the correct answer.**

| | |
|---|---|
| 1. sleeping bag ___ | a. We have a test at 9:00 on Monday morning! |
| 2. a bathing suit ___ | b. The river is filled with trout. |
| 3. insect repellent ___ | c. There's a nice pond. |
| 4. a fishing pole ___ | d. We're staying overnight. |
| 5. your homework ___ | e. The mosquitoes always come out at night. |

___ 5

## GIVE IT A TRY

**1. Complete the conversation with the correct responses. Write the letter of the correct answer.**

| | |
|---|---|
| 1. What's it used for? ___ | a. It's a garlic press. |
| 2. And then what? ___ | b. I'm glad to do it. |
| 3. How does it work? ___ | c. It's used to crush garlic. |
| 4. What's this thing? ___ | d. Then you put it in here and press down. |
| 5. Thanks for helping me. ___ | e. First, you peel the garlic. |

___ 5

**2. Complete each sentence with the letter of the correct answer.**

1. You'll need ________________ because you could get badly sunburned.
   a. a water bottle
   b. some sunscreen
   c. a barbie

2. What do I need ________________ for? Are there mosquitoes?
   a. an esky
   b. a knife
   c. insect repellent

3. We'll also need a ________________. It gets dark on the mountain.
   a. flashlight
   b. sunglasses
   c. fire extinguisher

4. Don't forget to take the ________________. We need it for our outdoor grill.
   a. candles
   b. drinks
   c. charcoal

5. Bring your sleeping bag. It's a ________________.
   a. one-day hiking trip
   b. weekend camping trip
   c. picnic

[ ] 5

# Unit 8 Test

TOTAL SCORE ___ 20

Name: ______________________ Date: ___________

## LISTEN TO THIS

Track 16

**1. A person is talking to a travel agent. Listen and check (✓) the correct answer.**

| | Wants | Doesn't want |
|---|---|---|
| 1. a package | | |
| 2. a single room | | |
| 3. a non-smoking room | | |
| 4. scuba diving | | |
| 5. cable TV | | |

___ 5

Track 17

**2. A hotel clerk is telling a guest when services are available in the hotel. Listen and write the letter of the correct answer.**

1. breakfast ___
2. yoga ___
3. the shuttle bus ___
4. the massage parlor ___
5. the swimming pool ___

a. 9:00 A.M.to 12:00 P.M.
b. Monday through Saturday
c. all day
d. 7:00 to 10:00 A.M.
e. 9:00 to 10:30 A.M.

___ 5

## GIVE IT A TRY

**1. Complete each sentence with the letter of the correct answer.**

1. I'd like to see pictures of the hotel. Do you have a ______________?
   a. tour
   b. brochure
   c. price

2. If you want to hike and scuba dive, a ______________ would be better.
   a. hotel
   b. package
   c. double room

3. Is the package deal ______________? We want to stay within our budget.
   a. friendly
   b. reasonable
   c. convenient

4. Yes, I'd like to ______________ a reservation at your hotel for next Friday.
   a. have
   b. take
   c. make

5. My husband needs to leave the hotel early. Could he get ______________, please?
   a. a wake-up call
   b. room service
   c. a get-up call

5

**2. Read each sentence and choose the correct response. Circle the letter of the correct answer.**

1. We'd like to check out, please.
   a. Do you have a reservation?
   b. Certainly, sir. I hope you enjoyed your stay.
   c. Take a look at this brochure.

2. Could I have a room with a view?
   a. Just call Room Service at extension 54.
   b. They'll send it up to your room.
   c. I'm sorry. Those rooms are all taken.

3. Could you tell me what time the restaurant opens?
   a. It opens at 8:00 A.M.
   b. It is closed now.
   c. It is open until 10:00 P.M.

4. I'd like to make a reservation, please.
   a. Here's your room key.
   b. For what dates?
   c. What are you interested in seeing?

5. Do you need any help with your suitcases?
   a. Yes, please. We don't manage.
   b. No, thanks. We are managers.
   c. No, thanks. We can manage.

5

# Unit 9 Test

TOTAL SCORE ___ 20

Name: ______________________________ Date: __________

## LISTEN TO THIS

Track 18

**1. People are talking about places to visit in Paris. Listen and write the letter of the correct answer.**

| | |
|---|---|
| 1. Champs-Elysées ___ | a. get an amazing view |
| 2. The Louvre ___ | b. take pictures |
| 3. The Eiffel Tower ___ | c. see the Mona Lisa |
| 4. The cafes ___ | d. try croissants |
| 5. The Seine ___ | e. go shopping |

___ 5

Track 19

**2. A clerk is talking to a visitor. Are these statements true or false? Listen and check (✓) the correct answer.**

| | True | False |
|---|---|---|
| 1. The impressionist gallery is on the third floor. | ☐ | ☐ |
| 2. The guided tour includes the whole museum. | ☐ | ☐ |
| 3. It's a two-hour tour. | ☐ | ☐ |
| 4. Lunch is provided. | ☐ | ☐ |
| 5. The tour costs $15.00 | ☐ | ☐ |

___ 5

## GIVE IT A TRY

**1. Complete each sentence with the letter of the correct answer.**

1. ____ the number 5 bus and take it to the last stop.
2. You have to ____ the train at the last stop.
3. When does the tour ____? I know it ends at 2:00.
4. When is this tour going to ____? I'm so tired!
5. We can get money when the bus ____ across from the bank.

a. start
b. stops
c. end
d. catch
e. get off

5

**2. Are these statements true or false? Check (✓) the correct answer.**

| | True | False |
|---|---|---|
| 1. Rain forests have historic buildings. | ☐ | ☐ |
| 2. You can go bird-watching in a tropical paradise. | ☐ | ☐ |
| 3. People go diving for buried treasure at a sidewalk cafe. | ☐ | ☐ |
| 4. You never find bargains at a street market. | ☐ | ☐ |
| 5. Brochures have information about places to visit. | ☐ | ☐ |

5

# Unit 10 Test

TOTAL SCORE ___ 20

Name: ______________________ Date: __________

## LISTEN TO THIS

Track 20

**1. People are describing their classmates. Match the subjects they study with their descriptions. Listen and write the letter of the correct answer.**

1. Engineering ___
2. Law ___
3. Art ___
4. Medicine ___
5. Business ___

a. the guy in the black shirt
b. the woman in the pink sweater
c. the man with the white beard
d. the one with the red hair and the blue jacket
e. the woman with the purple boots

___ 5

Track 21

**2. A woman is talking about her previous teachers. Did she like or dislike them? Listen and check (✓) the correct answer.**

| | Like | Dislike |
|---|---|---|
| 1. Mr. Sandburg | | |
| 2. Mrs. Chestnut | | |
| 3. Ms. Mitchell | | |
| 4. Mr. Higgins | | |
| 5. Mrs. Moon | | |

___ 5

## GIVE IT A TRY

**1. Read the dialogue and number the sentences in the correct order.**

1. ___ A: The one in the jean jacket.
2. ___ B: Which one?
3. ___ B: I think he's the one who just moved into my apartment building.
4. ___ A: Who's that guy?
5. ___ A: He's the one I'd like to meet.

___ 5

**2. Complete each sentence with letter of the correct answer.**

1. My boyfriend is quite ________________. He never pays for anything.
   a. stingy
   b. considerate
   c. aggressive

2. Delia's parents are not very ________________. They let her stay out late.
   a. outgoing
   b. strict
   c. open-minded

3. He's so ________________. He buys me flowers once a week.
   a. considerate
   b. honest
   c. hardworking

4. That man is so ________________! He never shares with anyone!
   a. moody
   b. honest
   c. greedy

5. Don't you wish Dad was more ________________? Then he wouldn't be afraid to ask his boss for a raise.
   a. aggressive
   b. stingy
   c. greedy

5

# Unit 11 Test

TOTAL SCORE ___ 20

Name: ______________________ Date: __________

## LISTEN TO THIS

Track 22

**1. Simon and Kazuo are talking about sports they have tried. Are these statements true or false? Listen and check (✓) the correct answer.**

| | True | False |
|---|---|---|
| 1. Simon is terrified of hang gliding. | ☐ | ☐ |
| 2. Kazuo has gone hang gliding many times. | ☐ | ☐ |
| 3. The last time Simon went hang gliding was in the summer. | ☐ | ☐ |
| 4. Kazuo enjoys hang gliding because it's exciting. | ☐ | ☐ |
| 5. Simon went bungee-jumping off a helicopter. | ☐ | ☐ |

___ 5

Track 23

**2. A woman is telling her friend a story. Are these statements true or false? Listen and check (✓) the correct answer.**

| | True | False |
|---|---|---|
| 1. The children locked the babysitter out of the house. | ☐ | ☐ |
| 2. The children started to laugh. | ☐ | ☐ |
| 3. The children weren't wearing any shoes. | ☐ | ☐ |
| 4. She used a rock to break the window. | ☐ | ☐ |
| 5. She spent her money on a new bicycle. | ☐ | ☐ |

___ 5

## GIVE IT A TRY

**1. Find the definition for each expression and circle the letter of the correct answer.**

1. *It was really cool* means
   a. it was quite cold.
   b. it was really enjoyable.
   c. it was really disappointing.

2. *I spent more time in the water than on the board* means
   a. I didn't surf well.
   b. I surfed pretty well.
   c. I decided to swim instead of surf.

3. *There's nothing like it!* means
   a. it's really frustrating.
   b. it's really boring.
   c. it's really interesting.

4. *Scary? You bet!* means
   a. it is terrifying.
   b. it isn't terrifying.
   c. it is a bit terrifying.

5. *You never get tired of that feeling* means
   a. it's a feeling you get bored of.
   b. it's a feeling you always enjoy.
   c. it's a feeling you never enjoy.

[ ] 5

**2. Read each question and choose the correct response. Write the letter of the correct answer.**

1. Did I ever tell you about the time I found $200? ____
2. Have you ever tried skiing? ____
3. What did you do first? ____
4. So, what happened next? ____
5. Have you ever tried a winter sport? ____

a. Yes, snowboarding.
b. No, what happened?
c. No, I've never done it.
d. I didn't know what to do.
e. After that, I went home.

[ ] 5

# Unit 12 Test

TOTAL SCORE ___ 20

Name: ______________________ Date: __________

## LISTEN TO THIS

Track 24

**1. Two friends are talking about movies they've seen. Do they agree or disagree? Listen and check (✓) the correct answer.**

| | Agree | Disagree |
|---|---|---|
| 1. *Those Hairy Eyeballs* | | |
| 2. *Love Forever* | | |
| 3. *The Hamburger That Ate Me* | | |
| 4. *The Table Tennis Champion* | | |
| 5. *Mr. Chocolate Bar* | | |

___ 5

**2. Listen to the conversation again and match the movies with the opinions. Write the letter of the correct answer.**

1. *Those Hairy Eyeballs* ___
2. *Love Forever* ___
3. *The Hamburger That Ate Me* ___
4. *The Table Tennis Champion* ___
5. *Mr. Chocolate Bar* ___

a. The story was so slow-moving.
b. Actually, I thought it was quite funny.
c. I thought it was a total waste of time.
d. It was romantic, fast-paced, and the story was awesome!
e. The acting was amazing.

___ 5

## GIVE IT A TRY

**1. People are talking about movies. Do they agree or disagree? Check (✓) the correct answer.**

| | Agree | Disagree |
|---|---|---|
| 1. A: I don't think violence in movies is that bad.<br>B: Well, if you ask me, I think it is a problem. | | |
| 2. A: That movie was a waste of time!<br>B: Oh, come on! | | |
| 3. A: The performance was quite terrible.<br>B: I want my money back. | | |
| 4. A: It was hard for me to sit through that movie.<br>B: I thought the special effects were terrific. | | |
| 5. A: That movie was so superficial.<br>B: It didn't deal with real-life issues at all. | | |

___ 5

**2.** **Complete each conversation with the letter of the correct answer.**

1. **A:** What did you think of the ballet performance?
   **B:** I fell asleep. It was so _______________.

   a. slow-moving
   b. entertaining
   c. violent

2. **A:** I thought that movie was too _______________.
   **B:** I agree. I cried for an hour after it ended.

   a. silly
   b. depressing
   c. interesting

3. **A:** I loved that movie. My heart was beating so fast when the girl opened the closet.
   **B:** I know! It was so _______________, I don't think I can sleep tonight.

   a. superficial
   b. boring
   c. scary

4. **A:** The show was quite _______________.
   **B:** Yeah, I laughed so much it hurt!

   a. funny
   b. realistic
   c. one-sided

5. **A:** Those actors looked exactly like chickens.
   **B:** Yes, the costumes were so _______________.

   a. violent
   b. fast-paced
   c. realistic

[ ] **5**

# ANSWER KEY

## Unit 1 Test

### LISTEN TO THIS 1

1. b
2. a
3. a
4. c
5. c

### GIVE IT A TRY 1

1. b
2. a
3. c
4. a
5. c

### LISTEN TO THIS 2

1. false
2. true
3. true
4. true
5. false

### GIVE IT A TRY 2

1. b
2. c
3. c
4. a
5. b

## Unit 2 Test

### LISTEN TO THIS 1

1. d
2. c
3. b
4. e
5. a

### GIVE IT A TRY 1

1. c
2. b
3. a
4. c
5. b

### LISTEN TO THIS 2

1. d
2. e
3. a
4. c
5. b

### GIVE IT A TRY 2

1. e
2. d
3. a
4. b
5. c

## Unit 3 Test

### LISTEN TO THIS 1

1. c
2. e
3. d
4. b
5. a

### GIVE IT A TRY 1

1. b
2. b
3. c
4. a
5. b

### LISTEN TO THIS 2

1. must
2. must
3. doesn't have to
4. doesn't have to
5. must

### GIVE IT A TRY 2

1. c
2. e
3. a
4. b
5. d

## Unit 4 Test

### LISTEN TO THIS 1

1. c
2. d
3. e
4. b
5. a

### GIVE IT A TRY 1

1. b
2. e
3. d
4. a
5. c

### LISTEN TO THIS 2

1. c
2. e
3. d
4. a
5. b

### GIVE IT A TRY 2

1. c
2. b
3. a
4. c
5. b

## Unit 5 Test

### LISTEN TO THIS 1

1. true
2. false
3. false
4. true
5. false

### GIVE IT A TRY 1

1. 5
2. 3
3. 2
4. 1
5. 4

### LISTEN TO THIS 2

1. d
2. c
3. a
4. e
5. b

### GIVE IT A TRY 2

1. c
2. b
3. c
4. b
5. c

## Unit 6 Test

### LISTEN TO THIS 1

1. e
2. c
3. d
4. b
5. a

### GIVE IT A TRY 1

1. b
2. b
3. a
4. b
5. c

### LISTEN TO THIS 2

1 d
2. c
3. a
4. e
5. b

### GIVE IT A TRY 2

1. true
2. false
3. true
4. true
5. false

## Unit 7 Test

### LISTEN TO THIS 1

1. 4
2. 3
3. 5
4. 1
5. 2

### GIVE IT A TRY 1

1. c
2. d
3. e
4. a
5. b

### LISTEN TO THIS 2

1. d
2. c
3. e
4. b
5. a

### GIVE IT A TRY 2

1. b
2. c
3. a
4. c
5. b

## Unit 8 Test

### LISTEN TO THIS 1

1. wants
2. doesn't want
3. wants
4. doesn't want
5. wants

### LISTEN TO THIS 2

1. d
2. e
3. a
4. c
5. b

### GIVE IT A TRY 1

1. b
2. b
3. b
4. c
5. a

### GIVE IT A TRY 2

1. b
2. c
3. a
4. b
5. c

## Unit 9 Test

### LISTEN TO THIS 1

1. e
2. c
3. a
4. d
5. b

### GIVE IT A TRY 1

1. d
2. e
3. a
4. c
5. b

### LISTEN TO THIS 2

1. false
2. true
3. false
4. false
5. true

### GIVE IT A TRY 2

1. false
2. true
3. false
4. false
5. true

## Unit 10 Test

### LISTEN TO THIS 1

1. d
2. e
3. b
4. a
5. c

### GIVE IT A TRY 1

1. 3
2. 2
3. 4
4. 1
5. 5

### LISTEN TO THIS 2

1. dislike
2. like
3. like
4. dislike
5. like

### GIVE IT A TRY 2

1. a
2. b
3. a
4. c
5. a

## Unit 11 Test

### LISTEN TO THIS 1

1. false
2. true
3. false
4. true
5. true

### GIVE IT A TRY 1

1. b
2. a
3. c
4. a
5. b

### LISTEN TO THIS 2

1. false
2. false
3. true
4. true
5. false

### GIVE IT A TRY 2

1. b
2. c
3. d
4. e
5. a

## Unit 12 Test

### LISTEN TO THIS 1

1. agree
2. disagree
3. agree
4. agree
5. disagree

### GIVE IT A TRY 1

1. disagree
2. disagree
3. agree
4. disagree
5. agree

### LISTEN TO THIS 2

1. e
2. a
3. b
4. c
5. d

### GIVE IT A TRY 2

1. a
2. b
3. c
4. a
5. c

# AUDIO SCRIPT

## Unit 1 Test

### LISTEN TO THIS

**Track 2**

**1**

D: This is a great picnic, isn't it?

C: It sure is. The hot dogs taste delicious.

D: They sure do. I think we've met before, haven't we?

C: I'm not sure. Do you go to City College?

D: No, but I work at the diner across the street.

C: I remember you now. You're a server. I see you there every Wednesday.

D: Yes, you always order a Greek salad and an iced tea.

C: That's right. Good to see you again. My name's Christine.

D: I'm Doug. Sorry I didn't recognize you.

C: Well, I usually wear a suit when I eat at that diner.

**Track 3**

**2**

M: Hi, Sally!

S: Hi! Mariko, this is my friend Alex. Alex, this is Mariko.

M: Hi, Alex. Nice to meet you.

A: Hi, Mariko. I've heard so much about you.

S: Mariko just got back from Brazil.

A: Really? What did you do there?

M: I went dancing every night.

S: You stayed there for a month, didn't you?

M: Yeah, I found a really cheap hotel.

A: I hear you're an amazing dancer.

M: I'm not bad. Do you dance?

A: Yes, I do. I dance whenever I can.

M: Actually, I'm going to go dancing this weekend. Do you want to come?

A: Sounds fantastic!

## Unit 2 Test

### LISTEN TO THIS

**Track 4**

**1**

1.

A: Do you know where I can buy some fresh vegetables?

B: You can try the supermarket on Clinton Street. It's about three blocks from here.

2.

A: Excuse me. Where can I check my e-mail?

B: Well, I think there's an Internet cafe next to that tall building.

3.

A: Just my luck! I got ketchup on my pants!

B: I could lend you a pair of mine.

A: Thanks, but I really need this pair. Do you know where I can get them cleaned?

B: I think there's a dry cleaner's in the shopping mall over there.

4.

A: I have the worst headache. Do you have any aspirin?

B: I'm afraid I don't.

A: Do you know of any pharmacies around here?

B: Yes. There's one on the corner.

5.

A: Excuse me. Where can I mail this package?

B: You can try the copy shop behind the pharmacy.

A: Oh, great! Thank you!

**Track 5**

**2**

1.

A: Hi. Can I help you find something?

B: Yes. Can you tell me where I can find the gift shop?

A: There's one on the second floor. Take the elevator up one flight.

B: Thank you so much!

2.

C: Excuse me, is there a bathroom here?

A: There's one on the ground floor, three rooms down on your left.

C: Thanks.

3.

A: Yes. How can I help you?

D: Where can I find the European paintings?

A: They're on the third floor. Take the elevator up two flights. When you exit the elevator, turn right. They're just past the black and white photography show.

D: Thanks.

4.

E: Excuse me. Where's the exit? I need to leave right away.

A: It's straight ahead, about three rooms down.

5.

A: Can I help you?

F: Can you tell me where I can find the Egyptian art?

A: It's on the lower level. Take the elevator down one flight.

F: Thank you.

## Unit 3 Test

### LISTEN TO THIS

#### Track 6

**1**

1.

A: Hello?

B: Hi, Mr. Miller. This is Vincent's classmate, Adam. Is he there, please?

A: I'm sorry. He's not here right now. Can I take a message?

B: Yes, please. I'm calling to tell him there's no school tomorrow. Classes are canceled.

A: Oh, OK. I'll tell him as soon as he gets in.

2.

A: Hello. Dave London speaking.

B: Hi, Mr. London. Is Andy there?

A: I'm afraid he isn't. Could I take a message?

B: Yes, please.

A: Just a moment. Let me get a pen. All right, go ahead.

B: Could you tell Andy I'm having a birthday party next Friday at my place at 8:00?

A: Sure. I'll give him that message. What's your name?

B: Oh, yeah. I forgot! It's Jimmy.

3.

A: Hello?

B: Hello, Dad. How are you?

A: I'm fine. Is everything OK with you?

B: Yeah... I just need to talk to Mom.

A: She went out, Laura. Do you want me to tell her something?

B: Yeah... just tell her to call me back when she gets a chance.

A: All right. I'll do that.

4.

A: Hello.

B: Hello. This is Fran's coworker, Ellen. Is this her husband?

A: Yes, it is. But she's not here right now. Is there anything I can help you with?

B: Can you tell Fran I can't pick her up tomorrow? My car won't start.

A: Oh, that's too bad. I'll tell her when she gets in.

5.

A: Hello. This is Betsy speaking. How can I help you?

B: Is your manager, Mr. Simpson there? I'd like to speak to him.

A: I'm sorry. He's in a meeting right now. Can I take a message?

B: Yes, please. This is Mrs. Simpson, his wife. Could you tell him I am angry at him for not calling me back?

#### Track 7

**2**

A: Good afternoon. Human resources department. Can I help you?

B: Yes, please. I'm interested in working as a security guard at your department store. Could you tell me how to apply?

A: Yes, of course. You just need to fill out a job application form and send it to us.

B: Great. Can you send me a form, please? My name is John DiCarlo and I live at 328 Saint Nick Street.

A: I'll need to know your city, state, and zip code, too.

B: Brooklyn, New York. 11215.

A: OK. We'll send that out to you right away.

B: I'd also like to apply for a credit card for your department store.

A: You'll have to speak to someone else about that. Hold on a moment, please. I'll see if he's available. I'm sorry. His line is busy now. You'll need to call back. The number is...

B: One moment, please. Let me get a pen. OK. Go ahead.

A: 718-658-0091. Please ask to speak to Charles.

B: Thank you very much.

## Unit 4 Test

### LISTEN TO THIS

#### Track 8

**1**

1.

A: Don't you think textbooks sold in the school bookstore are too expensive?

B: Yeah... sure I do. Students are too poor to pay for them. It's not very considerate.

A: What can the school do?

B: The school bookstore can have a book sale. How does that sound?

A: That sounds great!

2.

A: Is that your neighbor's stereo? It's really loud!

B: Sorry... I asked him to turn the volume down, but he refused to do it.

A: I have an idea! Let's call the police and complain that there's too much noise.

B: Leave it to you to think of that.

3.

A: It's really a problem when people bring their cell phones to class. It's not polite and it disturbs everyone.

B: I agree, but what can we do about it?

**A:** Let's have a sign that says, "If your cell phone rings, you fail the class."

**B:** That wouldn't work. It's not fair.

4.

**A:** There aren't enough computers in our classroom. It's a big problem.

**B:** I know! It's so annoying to share a computer with another student.

**A:** The student I shared a computer with today would not let me use it! What can I do about it?

**B:** You can set a time limit.

**A:** Good idea.

5.

**A:** The cafeteria is too expensive. I just spent five dollars on a hot dog. I could buy five of them on the street for the same price.

**B:** Let's start bringing our own lunch.

**A:** That's too risky. The last time I ate your cooking, it gave me a stomachache for three days.

### Track 9

**2**

1.

**A:** What's the problem?

**B:** My brother George is so noisy. He always plays his guitar while I'm studying.

**A:** Why don't you ask him to play outside?

**B:** That's a good idea. I haven't tried that.

2.

**A:** My brother Stan is so annoying. He always tells such stupid jokes whenever I bring home a friend.

**B:** Why don't you tell him he's not funny and ask him to stop embarrassing you in front of your friends?

**A:** I tried but he never listens.

3.

**A:** I have a problem and I don't know what to do. My little brother Wilbur sings in his sleep.

**B:** Well, is he a good singer?

**A:** No, he's terrible!

**B:** In that case, I think you should tell him to take singing lessons.

**A:** Good idea!

4.

**A:** Fred is the cheapest guy I've ever gone out with. He's your brother. What should I do?

**B:** I suppose you should tell him he's cheap. That's what I always do.

**A:** Oh, that's no good.

5.

**A:** My older brother Danny always talks on his cell phone when he's driving. What should I do?

**B:** If I were you, I'd tell him it's dangerous.

**A:** I suppose I should.

# Unit 5 Test

## LISTEN TO THIS

### Track 10

**1**

1.

**A:** Have you heard about Soo-jung?

**B:** No, I haven't spoken to her in a while. How are things with her?

**A:** Fantastic. She has her own TV show now.

2.

**A:** Hi, Kim. I have some great news.

**B:** Oh, yeah. What is it?

**A:** Valerie won the lottery. She's going to get three million dollars.

3.

**A:** Eun-mi is getting married to Hyun-jin!

**B:** You're kidding. What made her decide that?

**A:** I don't know. I guess she fell in love him.

4.

**A:** Have you heard about Anna?

**B:** I haven't talked to her since high school. What's happening with her?

**A:** She was in a car accident recently, but she only broke her ankle.

**B:** I'm glad it wasn't worse.

5.

**A:** Hey, Paul. Have you heard about Junko?

**B:** No, what's she doing these days?

**A:** She's going back to college to study law.

**B:** Good for her!

### Track 11

**2**

1.

**A:** Did you hear what happened to Becky?

**B:** No, what happened?

**A:** Well, let me tell you. She was driving too fast and she got a speeding ticket.

**B:** Oh, poor Becky. She should have driven slower.

2.

**A:** Did you hear about Sean? He was in the hospital.

**B:** Why did he go to the hospital?

**A:** He studied for 72 hours without sleep.

**B:** That's so crazy. He should have managed his time better. Is he OK?

**A:** Yeah, he's fine. But he missed his test.

3.

**A:** Where's Takeshi? I haven't seen him lately.

**B:** You didn't hear what happened, did you?

**A:** No, what happened?

**B:** His mother put out a display of glass vegetables and fruit in the living room. Anyway, Takeshi didn't realize and ended up breaking his tooth on a grape.

**A:** Unbelievable! He should have been more careful.

4.

A: Have you heard about Nancy? She missed her math test because she woke up late. Now she's going to fail the test.

B: That's so weird. She usually wakes up early. She should have set her alarm clock.

5.

A: Has Jeanie told you about her boyfriend Phil?

B: No, what happened?

A: Well, let me tell you. He tried to surprise Jeanie by asking her to marry him, but he forgot to put the ring in the box. He left it at the jewelry store.

B: That's crazy! He should have checked first.

## Unit 6 Test

### LISTEN TO THIS

**Track 12**

**1**

A: You look terrible. Are you OK?

B: To tell you the truth, I don't feel very well.

A: Why? What's the matter?

B: I have an awful backache.

A: Did you take anything for it?

B: I took some aspirin but it didn't help at all. I can't move so well.

A: Why didn't you call a doctor?

B: I thought I might feel better in a few hours. But I feel worse now.

A: Why don't you go home?

B: But I have an important meeting in a few minutes!

A: You'd better call the doctor and ask him what he thinks.

B: Maybe you're right.

**Track 13**

**2**

A: May I help you?

B: Yes, please. I don't feel well, but I can't miss work. What do you recommend?

A: What are your symptoms?

B: I have a terrible stomachache, headache, and a fever.

A: Well, that sounds like the flu. I recommend a non-prescription pain reliever and a fever reducer.

B: How often do I take it?

A: You should take one tablet every four to six hours.

B: Are there any special instructions?

A: You must take it with food.

B: Am I allowed to take aspirin with this medication?

A: No, you shouldn't take any aspirin.

B: Is coffee OK?

A: No, but you can have tea.

B: If the symptoms continue for more than 72 hours, should I keep taking them?

A: No. Definitely not. Then you had better see a doctor.

B: OK. I'll buy one package.

A: That'll be $9.00.

## Unit 7 Test

### LISTEN TO THIS

**Track 14**

**1**

Here's a fast and simple recipe for making a cheesecake. Totally delicious for dessert!

You'll need these ingredients: five packages of cream cheese, two eggs, a pint of heavy cream, five graham crackers, two cups of sugar, and a teaspoon of vanilla extract. You'll also need a nine-inch round pie pan and an electric mixer. Now, let's see if I can remember... Oh, yes. First, put the cream cheese, eggs, sugar, vanilla extract, and heavy cream into a bowl. Then mix it all together until it's smooth and creamy. After that, put the graham crackers in the pan and break them into very small pieces. Make sure there's enough to cover the whole pan. Next, pour the other ingredients over it. Finally, put it into the oven and bake it for 40 minutes at 230 degrees. When the top is lightly brown and crisp, it's ready.

**Track 15**

**2**

A: Hi, Yoshi, do you want to go on a camping trip with us next weekend?

B: Sure. What do I need to bring?

A: Well, for one thing, you need a sleeping bag.

B: Why do I need that?

A: We're staying overnight. And you might want to bring a bathing suit because there's a nice pond.

B: What else do I need?

A: You definitely need insect repellent. The mosquitoes always come out at night. And you should think about taking a fishing pole with you. The river is filled with trout.

B: Trout, what's that?

A: It's a type of fish! We're bringing an outdoor grill to cook them on.

B: Sounds delicious. Is there anything else I'll need to bring?

A: Yeah, you might want to bring your homework.

B: Are you crazy? What do I need my homework for?

A: We have a test at 9:00 on Monday morning!

## Unit 8 Test

### LISTEN TO THIS

#### Track 16

**1**

A: Can I help you?

B: Yes, can you recommend a hotel in Hawaii, please?

A: Are you interested in just a hotel or a package?

B: Well, a package would probably be better. I want to take surfing lessons.

A: I see. How many people are coming on this trip?

B: My wife and our five children.

A: I guess a single room won't be enough.

B: No, I'm afraid not. Could you make sure the room is non-smoking? My wife is very allergic to smoke.

A: Yes, certainly. Would you like your package to include scuba diving?

B: Well... I don't think so. Just surfing lessons. Oh... one more thing. Please make sure our room has cable TV. Our children can't live without it.

A: Yes, that's no problem.

#### Track 17

**2**

A: Excuse me. Can I still get some breakfast?

B: Yes, certainly. Our breakfast buffet is open from 7:00 to 10:00 A.M.

A: And do you know when the yoga class is this morning?

B: It's from 9:00 to 10:30 A.M.

A: Is there a shuttle bus that goes to the city?

B: Yes, it leaves every ten minutes. Unfortunately it's only available from 9:00 A.M. to 12:00 P.M.

A: Oh... that's too bad. Maybe I can stay in the hotel this afternoon and get a massage.

B: That sounds relaxing. The massage parlor is open all day.

A: Great! I think I'll have some breakfast, do some yoga, get a massage, and then go for a swim.

B: I'm sorry, ma'am. The pool is only available Monday through Saturday. And today is...

A: Sunday. That's OK. I'll go swimming tomorrow.

## Unit 9 Test

### LISTEN TO THIS

#### Track 18

**1**

S: Hey, Matt. I'm taking a trip to Paris next week. Didn't you live there?

M: Yes, for nine months.

S: Could you help me? I need some ideas for things to do.

M: Well, what are you interested in doing?

S: First, I want to go shopping.

M: Well, there are many specialty shops along the Champs-Elysées.

S: Sounds great. I'd also like to see the Mona Lisa.

M: Yes, you should definitely see it. It's in the Louvre. There's a lot of great art there.

S: I can't wait to see it. How about the Eiffel Tower?

M: Well, you shouldn't miss it. You can get an amazing view from the top.

S: What else is there to do? How about the cafes?

M: They are good places to relax and try a croissant. The croissants in France are so delicious.

S: Oh, I love croissants!

M: And one more thing…you can't miss a walk along the Seine.

S: That's the big river, right?

M: Yeah. It is a great place to take pictures.

S: I can't wait to get to Paris. It all sounds so exciting!

#### Track 19

**2**

A: Excuse me. Where is the impressionist gallery?

B: It's on the second floor. You know, there is a guided tour available.

A: Oh. What does the tour include?

B: It's a guided tour of the whole museum.

A: How long is it?

B: It's two and a half hours.

A: Is lunch provided?

B: I'm sorry. In fact, no food is allowed in the museum.

A: Oh. I didn't know that. I'd better get some lunch and come back.

B: That sounds like a good idea.

A: I have one more question. How much does it cost?

B: It's $15.00.

## Unit 10 Test

### LISTEN TO THIS

#### Track 20

**1**

A: I've been here nearly one month and I still don't know anyone in this school. Can you help me?

B: Sure.

A: Who's that guy in the black shirt?

B: I think his name is Sam. He's studying medicine.

A: Do you know who that woman in the pink sweater is?

B: That's Marge. She studies art.

A: Oh, yeah. I think I met her at registration. Who's she standing next to?

B: Which one? There are three people with her.

A: The man with the white beard.

B: That's Noah. He decided to return to school to study business.

A: Oh, interesting. Do you know who that man is?

B: The one with the red hair and the blue jacket? I'm not sure what his name is, but I know he studies engineering.

A: OK. And who's that woman standing on the other side of him?

**B:** The woman with the purple boots?

**A:** Yes, who's she? She's cute.

**B:** That's Leslie. She's studying law.

### Track 21

**2**

Mr. Sandburg was a pretty moody teacher. One minute, he was smiling at us and the next minute he was yelling at everybody for no reason at all. I was quite afraid of him. Mrs. Chestnut was a very considerate teacher. If you did your homework incorrectly, she never got angry. She just showed you how to do it again. Ms. Mitchell was quite strict, but I learned a lot in her class. In fact, I still remember everything she taught me. Mr. Higgins was really smart, but quite conceited. Every day he told us about all the books he wrote and all the awards he won and all the master's degrees he had, but he didn't teach us anything. Mrs. Moon was a really open-minded woman. She believed that women should be able to get the same jobs and amount of money as men. It's because of her I am now a successful lawyer.

## Unit 11 Test

### LISTEN TO THIS

### Track 22

**1**

**K:** Have you ever tried hang gliding, Simon?

**S:** No, I've never done it. Kazuo, have you?

**K:** Yes, I've done it lots of times. And it always scares me.

**S:** When was the last time you went hang gliding?

**K:** The last time was in the summer. It was terrifying.

**S:** If it's so scary, Kazuo, why do you do it?

**K:** Because it's so exciting! Have you ever tried a dangerous sport?

**S:** Yes, I have. I went bungee-jumping out of a helicopter over Taipei.

**K:** Was it fun?

**S:** I loved it!

### Track 23

**2**

**A:** Did I ever tell you about the time I got locked out of a house?

**B:** No, please tell me.

**A:** I was babysitting three children and their parents were out of town.

**B:** So, how did you get locked out?

**A:** The children wanted to go outside and play. When we walked outside, the door closed behind us and I realized I didn't have a key.

**B:** Oh, no. Then what happened?

**A:** The children became scared and they all started to cry. It was getting cold outside, and they weren't wearing any shoes. I began to panic.

**B:** That sounds awful. What did you do next?

**A:** I broke a window with a rock and crawled inside the house. The children thought it was great. They cheered when I let them inside.

**B:** Wow! Were you hurt?

**A:** I had a few cuts from the glass, but that's not the worst part of the story.

**B:** What do you mean? What else happened?

**A:** I spent most of the money I made babysitting to fix the broken window!

## Unit 12 Test

### LISTEN TO THIS

### Track 24

**1**

**A:** Thanks for returning *Those Hairy Eyeballs*. What did you think of it?

**B:** I thought it was great.

**A:** So did I. The acting was amazing. I cried when the hairy eyeball monster fell in love with the woman. Did you watch the other four movies?

**B:** Yes. I'll give them back to you tomorrow.

**A:** Please don't rush. So, did you like them?

**B:** Well...some of them. I didn't like a couple of them at all.

**A:** Which ones?

**B:** I hated *Love Forever*.

**A:** Really? What didn't you like about it? I thought it was wonderful.

**B:** The story was so slow-moving, I fell asleep watching it.

**A:** It wasn't slow-moving! It was suspenseful!

**B:** Sorry, but I disagree. What's your opinion about *The Hamburger That Ate Me*? You probably didn't like it because it wasn't suspenseful at all.

**A:** Actually, I thought it was quite funny.

**B:** Oh, yeah? I thought so, too. I laughed through the whole film. So, how did you feel about *The Table Tennis Champion*?

**A:** I thought it was a total waste of time.

**B:** What didn't you like about it?

**A:** The main idea. It was so superficial.

**B:** Yeah. That's true. The idea of a man leaving his wife to play table tennis is pretty stupid.

**A:** What did you think of *Mr. Chocolate Bar*?

**B:** I didn't like it at all.

**A:** You didn't? I loved it. It was the best movie I've seen all year. It was romantic, fast-paced, and the story was awesome!

**B:** In my opinion, the story was confusing. Who ever heard of a woman falling in love with a chocolate bar?

**A:** Personally, I thought it was very creative.

# TRACK LIST

| TRACK | CONTENT |
|---|---|
| 1 | Title and copyright |
| 2 | Unit 1, Listen to This 1 |
| 3 | Unit 1, Listen to This 2 |
| 4 | Unit 2, Listen to This 1 |
| 5 | Unit 2, Listen to This 2 |
| 6 | Unit 3, Listen to This 1 |
| 7 | Unit 3, Listen to This 2 |
| 8 | Unit 4, Listen to This 1 |
| 9 | Unit 4, Listen to This 2 |
| 10 | Unit 5, Listen to This 1 |
| 11 | Unit 5, Listen to This 2 |
| 12 | Unit 6, Listen to This 1 |

| TRACK | CONTENT |
|---|---|
| 13 | Unit 6, Listen to This 2 |
| 14 | Unit 7, Listen to This 1 |
| 15 | Unit 7, Listen to This 2 |
| 16 | Unit 8, Listen to This 1 |
| 17 | Unit 8, Listen to This 2 |
| 18 | Unit 9, Listen to This 1 |
| 19 | Unit 9, Listen to This 2 |
| 20 | Unit 10, Listen to This 1 |
| 21 | Unit 10, Listen to This 2 |
| 22 | Unit 11, Listen to This 1 |
| 23 | Unit 11, Listen to This 2 |
| 24 | Unit 12, Listen to This 1 and 2 |